S.S.F. Public Library
Grand Ave.
306 Walnut Ave.
South San Francisco, CA 94080

Y0-BYZ-789

MAR 2 0

EXPLORING EARTH'S BIOMES

TUNDRA BIOMES
AROUND THE WORLD

by Phillip Simpson

Content consultant:
Rosanne W. Fortner
Professor Emeritus
The Ohio State University
Columbus, OH

CAPSTONE PRESS
a capstone imprint

Fact Finders Books are published by Capstone Press
1710 Roe Crest Drive, North Mankato, Minnesota 56003
www.capstonepub.com

Copyright © 2020 by Capstone Press, a Capstone imprint. All rights reserved.
No part of this publication may be reproduced in whole or in part, or stored in a
retrieval system, or transmitted in any form or by any means, electronic, mechanical,
photocopying, recording, or otherwise, without written permission of the publisher.

Library of Congress Cataloging-in-Publication Data
Names: Simpson, Phillip W., 1971–author.
Title: Tundra Biomes Around the World / by Phillip Simpson.
Description: North Mankato, Minnesota: Capstone Press, [2020] | Series:
   Fact Finders. Exploring Earth's Biomes | Includes index. | Audience: Age
   8–9. | Audience: Grade 4 to 6.
Identifiers: LCCN 2019002048| ISBN 9781543572353 (hardcover) | ISBN
   9781543575361 (paperback) | ISBN 9781543572377 (ebook pdf)
Subjects: LCSH: Tundra ecology—Juvenile literature.
Classification: LCC QH541.5.T8 S49 2020 | DDC 577.5/86—dc23
LC record available at https://lccn.loc.gov/2019002048

Editorial Credits
Gina Kammer, editor; Julie Peters, designer; Morgan Walters, media researcher;
Kathy McColley, production specialist

Photo Credits
Alamy: Megapress, 25, P.A. Lawrence, LLC., 24, Renato Granieri, 9; iStockphoto:
aaprophoto, 16, RelaxedPace, 17; Newscom: Eric Baccega/agefotostock, 18, SABRINA
BLANCHARD, JONATHAN WALTER, JONATHAN STOREY AFP, 27, SOPHIE
RAMIS, ALAIN BOMMENEL AFP, 28, Ton Koene/agefotostock/, 19; Science Source:
Gary Hincks, bottom 8; Shutterstock: Andy Fogelsonger, spread 18, spread 20-21,
David Dennis, bottom left 4, 12, Denis Burdin, spread 26-27, spread 28-29, Designua,
top 5, evgenii mitroshin, 20, Galyna Andrushko, 11, Gregory A. Pozhvanov, (tundra)
Cover, bottom left 10, Grezova Olga, 13, indukas, 15, Natalia Davidovich, (moss) design
element throughout, nenets, spread 22-23, spread 24-25, nubephoto, (man) Cover, Peter
Hermes Furian, bottom left 6, Tatiana Gasich, 21, Troutnut, spread 10-11, spread 12-13,
spread 14-15, spread 16-17, ugljesa, bottom 7, Vladimir Melnik, spread 4-5, spread 6-7,
spread 8-9, Vladimir Melnikov, 23, Volodymyr Burdiak, 14

All internet sites appearing in back matter were available and accurate
when this book was sent to press.

Printed and bound in the USA.
PA70

TABLE OF CONTENTS

CHAPTER 1

FROZEN GROUND

Before you is a bare wasteland, frozen and hard. Not a single tree is in sight. The freezing wind threatens to blow you over. It chills you to the bone. Where are you? You're in the tundra.

Tundras are one of the five main biomes. These large areas have certain types of climates, plants, and animals. The five main biomes are aquatic, forest, desert, grassland, and tundra. Tundras are the coldest biomes on Earth and are mostly treeless. The tundra biome covers almost 10 percent of Earth's surface.

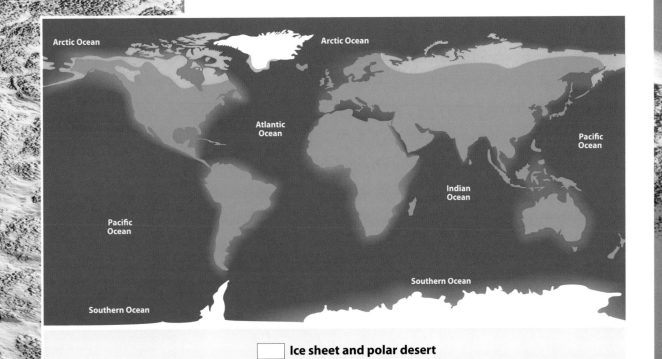

Ice sheet and polar desert
Tundra

The tundra biome features large areas of bare ground and rock. Short plants such as mosses, **lichens**, and small scrub cover the ground. Few humans or animals live in this biome because of the cold and lack of food. However, the few plants and animals living in tundras have **adapted** to the unique conditions and couldn't survive elsewhere. The three types of tundras are Arctic tundra, Antarctic tundra, and alpine tundra.

adapt—to change in order to survive; a change in an animal or plant to better fit its environment is called an adaptation
lichen—a flat, mosslike plant; it is made up of a kind of algae and a fungus that grow together

ARCTIC TUNDRA

The Arctic tundra is found in the Arctic Circle and the areas surrounding the North Pole. The Arctic tundra covers parts of northern Europe, Asia, and North America. These regions are very cold. The Arctic tundra has average temperatures as low as minus 30 degrees Fahrenheit (minus 34 degrees Celsius) in the winter months. In summer, the temperature in the Arctic tundra rises only to about 50°F (10°C). The Arctic subsoil—the area directly beneath the topsoil—is always frozen. This soil layer is called **permafrost**. It also contains frozen water.

WINTER SOLSTICE
(December 21 or 22)

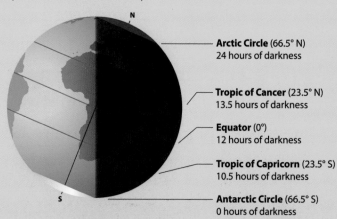

Arctic Circle (66.5° N)
24 hours of darkness

Tropic of Cancer (23.5° N)
13.5 hours of darkness

Equator (0°)
12 hours of darkness

Tropic of Capricorn (23.5° S)
10.5 hours of darkness

Antarctic Circle (66.5° S)
0 hours of darkness

FACT:
The winter solstice in the northern hemisphere is the moment when the sun is farthest from the north pole. However, people often recognize the winter solstice as the full 24-hour day.

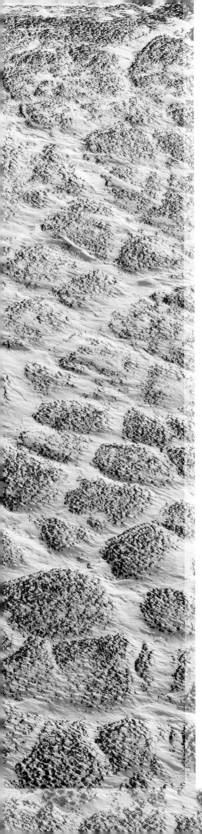

ANTARCTIC TUNDRA

The Antarctic tundra covers the smallest area of land. It's found on the continent of Antarctica as well as several nearby islands, including South Georgia and South Sandwich islands. On the Antarctic Peninsula, only small areas of rocky soil support tundra and permafrost. The rest of Antarctica is mostly covered by ice fields. It's too dry and cold for plant life. Average annual temperatures in the Antarctic are –56°F (–49°C).

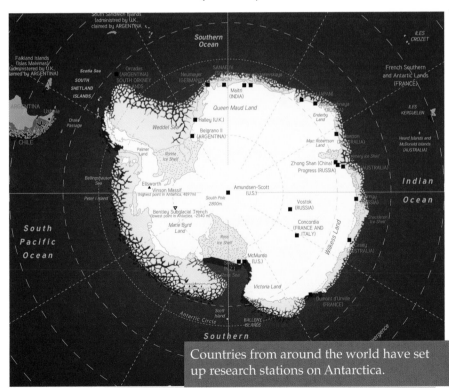

Countries from around the world have set up research stations on Antarctica.

permafrost—a layer of soil, usually below the topsoil, permanently frozen during both winter and summer

7

ALPINE TUNDRA

Alpine tundra is found above the **timberline** on high mountains all around the world. The climate is too cold and windy at these levels for trees to grow. Alpine tundra only extends to the snow line, which is always covered in snow—even in summer. However, compared to the other types of tundras, the alpine tundra has a longer growing season. Temperatures range up to about 50°F (10°C) in summer to well below freezing in winter. Alpine tundra usually has no permafrost.

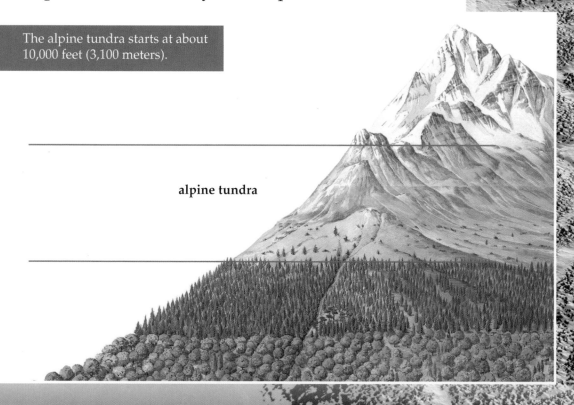

The alpine tundra starts at about 10,000 feet (3,100 meters).

alpine tundra

FACT:
The word tundra comes from people from Finland, who called their cold treeless areas "tunturia," meaning treeless plain.

timberline—the point on mountainsides beyond which trees do not grow

CHAPTER 2

HARDY **PLANTS** AND **ANIMALS**

Tundra plants and animals are hardy. They have to be! The frozen ground, cold weather, and windy landscape require unique features for survival. But tundra plants and animals are up to the challenge.

FACT:
The Arctic tundra has about 1,700 types of plants. Most are small and are sometimes called "ground cover" because they cover the ground.

TUNDRA PLANT LIFE

Antarctic and Arctic plant life are similar, with many types of lichens, grasses, liverworts, and mosses. Plants are unable to push roots deep into the frozen ground. For that reason, it's difficult for large plants such as trees to survive. Tundra plants have adapted to the high winds and the frozen soil. They are small and grow low to the ground. They group together and spread their roots over a wide area. Some plants in the Arctic tundra grow under a layer of snow.

The most common type of grass in the Arctic tundra is cotton grass.

Plants in the alpine tundra are similar to those in the Arctic tundra. They have almost identical **environmental** conditions. Similar to the Arctic tundra, shrubs, mosses, and lichens are plentiful. Alpine tundra grasses include tough tussock grass. This grass survives by quickly growing long roots.

Plants found in Greenland's tundra include grasses, bearberry, red algae, and mosses.

environmental—relating to the natural world and the impact of human activity on its condition

caribou moss

A common alpine tundra plant is the caribou moss, which is actually a type of lichen. Caribou moss can survive for a long time without water. It dries out and then starts to grow again when there is water.

Many flowering plants have thick hairs on their stems and leaves. The hairs protect them from harsh winds. Some plants have adapted by taking longer to form flower buds. They survive the winter below the soil's surface. They then emerge during the few weeks of summer to open and spread their seeds.

TUNDRA ANIMAL LIFE

Animals in the tundra have adapted to its extreme temperatures and tolerate long, cold winters. Their young are born and grow up in summer to avoid the harsh winter. Some **hibernate** in winter when food is scarce.

The brown bear is one of the few mammals that live in the Arctic tundra all year long. During summer, it stores up food as a layer of fat underneath its skin. The fat keeps the bear warm and is converted into energy. The energy keeps the bear alive in winter when it goes into the deep sleep of hibernation.

brown bear

musk ox

The musk ox also lives in the Arctic tundra for the entire year. Its coat has a short layer and a long layer of fur. Air trapped between these fur layers is warmed by body heat. The trapped air acts as **insulation** from the cold. The long fur protects the animal from wind and water. The musk ox's large, hard hooves allow it to break ice and drink the water below during winter.

hibernate—to go into a resting state over the winter, as if in a deep sleep
insulation—a material that stops heat, sound, or cold from entering or escaping

A number of **herbivores** survive in the Arctic tundra because of its plant life. Most tundra birds and mammals don't live there year-round. They use the tundra as a summer home. Many birds eat the plants that grow in summer. They then leave for warmer climates in winter.

Unlike the Arctic tundra, the Antarctic tundra doesn't have many animal species, as the tundra areas are so small. The animals that do make their homes there include seals, penguins, hares, and albatross.

albatross near Antarctica

caribou

Animals in the alpine tundra include mammals such as caribou. The caribou have adapted to this region by being able to survive on lichen. They have **microorganisms** in their stomachs that let them eat lichen. Very few other animals eat lichen. Scientists think that the caribou have evolved to eat lichen when other animals couldn't.

herbivore—an animal that eats only plants
microorganism—a living thing too small to be seen without a microscope

CHAPTER 3

HUMAN SURVIVORS

Tundra biomes are cold, harsh, and remote regions. Would you want to live in such a region? Some people do! Few people have settled in these places, compared to other biomes. However, evidence suggests that humans have lived in tundra regions for more than 20,000 years.

A teenage Nenet girl stands by her tent in Yamal, Russia.

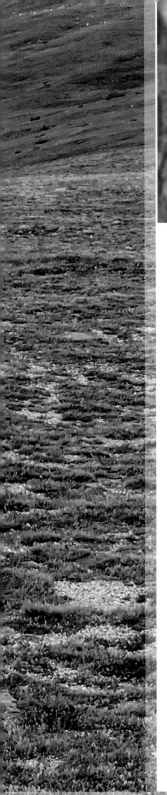

A young Inuit boy lives in Gjoa Haven, Canada. Intuits hunt animals including polar bears, fish, and Arctic hares.

Early humans may have been forced into the tundra from milder areas by other humans. Perhaps they moved into the tundra areas because there weren't as many people. This meant less **competition** for food and water. Many of these people were **nomadic**, following herds of animals. Today, many people in tundra areas, such as those in Alaska, live in permanent villages and towns. They deal with the same things most other people do in winter, including problems such as frozen pipes!

The largest human group in the tundra is the Inuit people. They live in the Arctic tundra in places such as Canada and Greenland. The Inuit live near the coast where they hunt caribou, seal, fish, and even the occasional whale. They make **traditional** clothing out of caribou skins and fur, just as their ancestors did.

competition—a situation in which two or more people are trying to get the same thing
nomadic—traveling from place to place in search of food and water
traditional—relating to customs that are handed down

The Innu are First Nations people who live in the tundra areas of northern Labrador and Quebec in Canada. The tundra environment once provided all they needed to survive. They hunted caribou for food and to make clothing and tools. Because of overhunting by other settlers, the numbers of caribou shrank over time. This led to the starvation of many of the Innu people. Many who survived were forced to move out of these areas.

A young boy dresses in thick, warm clothing in the Arctic tundra.

FACT:
Tundra regions are also popular with tourists. The combination of wildlife, amazing scenery, and few humans make tundras great for hunting, hiking, camping, and wildlife watching.

The Yakut live in the tundra in the Russian region of Siberia. Fishing is an important part of the Yakut economy. They eat some of the fish and sell the rest. They hunt for animal furs for clothing and to sell. The Yakut also breed hardy horses and cattle. The Yakut are nomadic and move twice a year—during summer to store hay and in winter for shelter.

A group of young Yakuts dress in traditional clothing and hold plates of foods in Yakutsk, Russia.

Other people have traveled to tundras for their natural resources, even though they are remote and hard to reach. Oil, natural gas, petroleum, and uranium are mined in these regions.

First Nations—any of the indigenous peoples or Indian communities of Canada, especially one formally recognized by the Canadian government

CHAPTER 4

THE HUMAN THREAT

The tundra biome is a valued and important **ecosystem**. This biome gives tourists the opportunity to see unique plants and animals or enjoy winter sports such as skiing. People also mine valuable oil and resources. However, people have greatly impacted the tundra wilderness by building homes, ski resorts, mines, and roads. Hunting has affected animal life. In addition, searching and drilling for oil has polluted the environment and threatened wildlife. Other threats include erosion and pesticides used to control insects.

Tundra doesn't grow back quickly if disturbed. For example, vehicles damage the tundra and the plants on its surface. The vehicle tracks remain for decades. Construction of roads and buildings can also damage this biome.

The hunt for **fossil fuels** is particularly damaging in the Arctic tundra. It's difficult to build pipelines through the permafrost. Large areas of tundra in the paths of pipelines are destroyed. In addition, oil or gas pipelines can break. The spilled fuel can kill wildlife and damage the ecosystem.

an oil field in western Siberia

ecosystem—a system of living and nonliving things in an environment
fossil fuels—fuels such as oil, coal, and natural gas made from decayed plants and animals that have been converted by heat and pressure in Earth's crust over hundreds of millions of years

Global warming is the greatest threat to tundra biomes. Humans continue to release **greenhouse gases** into the atmosphere. These gases are contributing to the heating of the planet. They create a barrier in Earth's atmosphere that keeps heat from escaping.

Global warming has already changed the tundra ecosystems. Temperatures have risen. With the rising temperatures, tundra fires have increased. Dead plants and peat, a type of decayed plant material, are extremely **flammable**.

a fire burning in the Alaska tundra

flammable—likely to catch fire
global warming—the increase in the average temperature of Earth's climate
greenhouse gas—a gas in a planet's atmosphere that traps heat energy from the sun; most greenhouse gases are water vapor, carbon dioxide, methane, nitrous oxide, and ozone

24

a forest destroyed by a fire in James Bay, Quebec, Canada

These fires reduce ground cover such as lichens, which the caribou need to survive. Fewer lichens and other plants will eventually impact animal life. With no food, tundra animals will become threatened and perhaps face extinction.

FACT:
Fires are not uncommon in the tundra. Lightening from a storm caused nearly 35 acres (14 hectares) of land to burn in 2018 near Talkeetna, Alaska.

CHAPTER 5

THE **FUTURE** OF **TUNDRAS**

Scientists believe that **climate change** and global warming will continue. In some regions, the temperature may be 12.6°F to 14.4°F (7°C to 8°C) warmer by the end of this century than it was in the 1950s. That means that some plant and animal species found only in tundra areas may become extinct.

Tundras will become wetter and warmer. Scientists believe that Arctic tundras will be warm enough to support larger plants and trees by 2050. This climate will be more suitable for different types of plants and animals not normally found in tundras.

climate change—a significant change in Earth's climate over a period of time

26

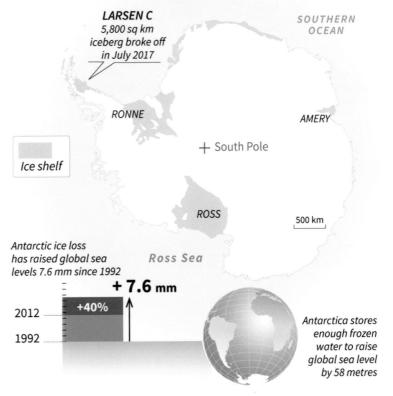

Sea levels rise as Antarctic melt accelerates

Rate of ice loss tripled since 2012 to 219 billion tonnes per year

LARSEN C
5,800 sq km
iceberg broke off
in July 2017

SOUTHERN OCEAN

RONNE

AMERY

+ South Pole

Ice shelf

ROSS

500 km

Antarctic ice loss
has raised global sea
levels 7.6 mm since 1992

Ross Sea

+ 7.6 mm

+40%

2012

1992

Antarctica stores
enough frozen
water to raise
global sea level
by 58 metres

As temperatures rise, polar ice melts
and sea levels rise.

While this may sound good for other species, it isn't so good for native plants and animals in tundra regions. They will face extinction. It's estimated that the tundra will decrease by 33 to 44 percent by the end of this century. One study shows that perhaps as much as 77 percent of the tundra will be gone by 2100.

The fate of permafrost is also a future concern. Tundra biomes store large amounts of dead organic matter, or carbon, in the frozen soil. Some of this matter has been frozen for thousands of years. Rising temperatures will thaw the permafrost. The organic material will begin to decay. As it does, it will release carbon dioxide into the atmosphere in the form of greenhouse gases.

Permafrost

■ Continuous cover　■ Discontinuous　■ Sporadic　■ Isolated

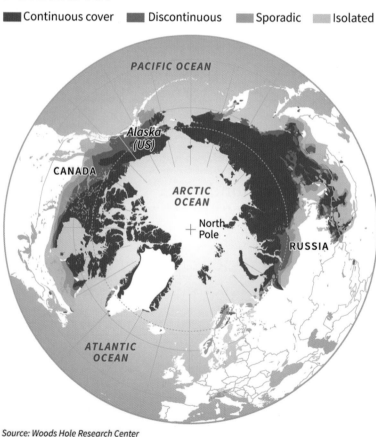

PACIFIC OCEAN

Alaska (US)

CANADA

ARCTIC OCEAN

+ North Pole

RUSSIA

ATLANTIC OCEAN

Source: Woods Hole Research Center

Permafrost (perenially frozen ground) covers about

25%

of land in the Northern Hemisphere

It contains about

1,500 billion tonnes

of carbon

2 x more than is in the atmosphere

CH_4

CO_2

Timebomb

When permafrost thaws it releases carbon into the atmosphere in the form of carbon dioxide (CO_2) and methane (CH_4).

These greenhouse gases accelerate global warming, which then speeds up the permafrost thaw.

© *AFP*

FACT:
What can you do to help? Less demand for fossil fuels will help preserve the tundra. Use solar energy in your home. Ask adults about installing solar panels. Do simple things to save energy such as turning off lights when you leave a room.

Greenhouse gases speed the thawing and add to global warming. If global warming continues as scientists believe it will, these biomes face destruction. The wildlife could become extinct. People living in the tundra will face problems as well. Melting permafrost causes roads and houses to sink. Pipelines could buckle and break.

However, reducing greenhouse gases can help protect Earth's tundra habitats. People can switch to energy such as solar and wind. Creating reserves and protected tundra areas to reduce human impact can also help. Conservation efforts would limit construction of roads, mines, and pipelines. It's up to everyone to work together to preserve this unique biome.

GLOSSARY

adapt (uh-DAPT)—to change in order to survive; a change in an animal or plant to better fit its environment is called an adaptation

climate change (KLY-muht CHAYNJ)—a significant change in Earth's climate over a period of time

competition (kahm-puh-TI-shuhn)—a situation in which two or more people are trying to get the same thing

ecosystem (EE-koh-sis-tuhm)—a system of living and nonliving things in an environment

environmental (in-vy-ruhn-MUHNT-uhl)—relating to the natural world and the impact of human activity on its condition

First Nations (FUHRST NAY-shuns)—any of the indigenous peoples or Indian communities of Canada, especially one formally recognized by the Canadian government

flammable (FLA-muh-buhl)—likely to catch fire

fossil fuels (FAH-suhl FYOOLZ)—fuels such as oil, coal, and natural gas made from decayed plants and animals that have been converted by heat and pressure in Earth's crust over hundreds of millions of years

global warming (GLOH-buhl WARM-ing)—the increase in the average temperature of Earth's climate

greenhouse gas (GREEN-houss GASS)—a gas in a planet's atmosphere that traps heat energy from the sun; most greenhouse gases are water vapor, carbon dioxide, methane, nitrous oxide, and ozone

herbivore (HUR-buh-vor)—an animal that eats only plants

hibernate (HYE-bur-nate)—to go into a resting state over the winter, as if in a deep sleep

insulation (in-suh-LAY-shun)—a material that stops heat, sound, or cold from entering or escaping

lichen (LYE-ken)—a flat, mosslike plant; it is made up of a kind of algae and a fungus that grow together

microorganism (mye-kro-OR-gan-iz-um)—a living thing too small to be seen without a microscope

nomadic (noh-MAD-ik)—traveling from place to place in search of food and water

permafrost (PUR-muh-frawst)—a layer of soil, usually below topsoil, permanently frozen during both winter and summer

timberline (TIM-bur-lyne)—the point on mountainsides beyond which trees do not grow

traditional (truh-DISH-uhn-uhl)—relating to customs that are handed down

READ MORE

Biskup, Agnieszka. *Exploring Ecosystems with Max Axiom, Super Scientist: 4D an Augmented Reading Science Experience.* Graphic Science 4D. North Mankato, MN: Capstone Press, 2019.

Boothroyd, Jennifer. *Let's Visit the Tundra.* Biome Explorers. Minneapolis: Lerner Publications, 2017.

Johansson, Philip. *The Tundra: Discover This Frozen Biome.* Discover the World's Biomes. Berkeley Heights, NJ: Enslow Elementary, 2015.

Schuetz, Kari. *Life in a Tundra.* Biomes Alive! Minneapolis: Bellwether Media, Inc., 2016.

INTERNET SITES

The Tundra Biome
http://www.ucmp.berkeley.edu/glossary/gloss5/biome/tundra.html

Tundra
http://www.newworldencyclopedia.org/entry/Tundra

Tundra: What Are Tundras?
https://www.nationalgeographic.com/environment/habitats/tundra-biome

CRITICAL THINKING QUESTIONS

1. What are the pros and cons of human influence in the tundra? Do you think humans are justified in exploring and utilizing the resources in the tundra? Use evidence to explain your thinking.
2. Why is the permafrost so important? What will happen if the permafrost melts?
3. Name the ways plants and animals have adapted to extreme environments such as the tundra. Why is it necessary for plants and animals to adapt to an environment?

INDEX